SPOTLIGHT ON NATURE
MONKEY

MELISSA GISH

CREATIVE EDUCATION • CREATIVE PAPERBACKS

Published by Creative Education and Creative Paperbacks
P.O. Box 227, Mankato, Minnesota 56002
Creative Education and Creative Paperbacks are imprints
of The Creative Company
www.thecreativecompany.us

Design by Chelsey Luther; production by Colin O'Dea
Art direction by Rita Marshall
Printed in the United States of America

Photographs by Alamy (CNM_456, imageBROKER, David Kleyn, Nature
Picture Library, B. O'Kane, CORREIA Patrice), Getty Images (Nadir Abra-
ham/EyeEm, ahteng, ASO FUJITA/amanaimagesRF, Jesse Kraft/EyeEm,
Giedrius Stakauskas/EyeEm), iStockphoto (4FR, abzerit, Antonel, archives,
davidevison, GlobalP, JanMengr, KeithSzafranski, Mark Kostich, LiliGraphie,
MikeLane45, miroslav_1, NTCo, outcast85, Photocech, plasmatic-t2, Sylvie-
Bouchard, Viktor_Kitaykin, winyoo08)

Library of Congress Cataloging-in-Publication Data
Names: Gish, Melissa, author.
Title: Monkey / Melissa Gish.
Series: Spotlight on nature.
Includes index.
Summary: A detailed chronology of developmental milestones drives this life
study of monkeys, including their habitats, physical features, and conserva-
tion measures taken to protect these primates.
Identifiers: ISBN 978-1-64026-342-0 (hardcover) / ISBN 978-1-62832-
874-5 (pbk) / ISBN 978-1-64000-484-9 (eBook)
This title has been submitted for CIP processing under LCCN 2020902418.

First Edition HC 9 8 7 6 5 4 3 2 1
First Edition PBK 9 8 7 6 5 4 3 2 1

CONTENTS

SNOW MONKEYS

of Jōshin'etsu-kōgen National Park

Japan is made up of 6,852 islands. The largest of these islands is Honshū. Here, a mountainous area slightly smaller than the city of Houston, Texas, has been set aside for wildlife. Golden eagles fly through treetops, while Japanese weasels scurry for safety. A solitary Japanese serow treks through the dense woodland. The goat-like animal stops to snuffle through leaf litter in search of acorns that the park's Asiatic black bears may have missed.

It is early May, and brilliantly pink cherry blossoms cover the sakura trees. A troop of Japanese macaques (muh-KAKS), or snow monkeys, has gathered by the Yokoyu River. As youngsters chase each other, adults rest in the shade. One female moves away from the group. For five and a half months, a baby has been growing inside her body. Now it is time to find a place to give birth.

CLOSE-UP
Vocalizing

Some monkeys use a range of unique sounds to "talk." For example, the green monkey uses distinct cries to warn of different predators such as snakes, leopards, or eagles. Its neighbor, the western red colobus monkey, understands and responds to those calls.

CHAPTER ONE
LIFE BEGINS

Monkeys are primates with slender bodies, long arms and legs, snouts, and forward-facing eyes. Most monkeys have tails, though some tails are very short. Highly developed brains enable monkeys to solve problems, use tools, and teach others how to perform tasks. The roughly 200 monkey species are divided into 2 groups: Old World and New World. Old World monkeys are native to Africa and Asia. New World monkeys inhabit the tropical forests of the Americas.

Some monkeys mate seasonally, while others reproduce year round. Depending on the species, monkeys can become parents by age four to seven. Their gestation period varies by size. Southern Africa's chacma baboons, males of which can weigh about 70 pounds (31.8 kg) as adults, take around 186 days to develop. Smaller than

JŌSHIN'ETSU-KŌGEN SNOW MONKEY MILESTONES

DAY ①

- ▸ Born
- ▸ Covered with dark fur
- ▸ Weight: 16 ounces (454 g)
- ▸ Height: 6 inches (15.2 cm)

Teeth

Chisel-like front incisors snip pieces of food.
Sharp, pointed canines pierce and rip.
Premolars and molars crush and grind food.
Monkeys' baby teeth fall out and are replaced
by permanent teeth at two to four years of age.

— FEATURED FAMILY —

Welcome to the World

The female snow monkey keeps quiet so as not to alert any predators that might be lurking in the area. She also wants to stay hidden from other monkeys, particularly jealous females who may want to steal the infant from her. Concealed behind a tree, she spends several minutes pushing. Soon, a tiny head appears. The mother reaches down and grasps her infant's shoulders, guiding him out of the birth canal. She immediately pulls him forward and begins licking his soft fur clean.

baboons, macaque species average 165 days. Weighing less than a stick of butter, the pygmy marmoset is the world's smallest monkey. This New World monkey's gestation period lasts about 134 days. Most monkeys give birth to one infant, but marmosets and tamarins always have twins or triplets.

Monkeys can be found in diverse habitats, from dense rainforests and snowy mountains to windswept grasslands and arid deserts. The northernmost monkey, the Japanese macaque, is capable of living in more than three feet (0.9 m) of snow in temperatures as low as 5 °F (-15 °C). Europe's only wild monkeys, a small population of tailless Barbary macaques, live in the British territory of Gibraltar. The two dozen or so marmoset species rarely leave the trees. Their chisel-like teeth scrape holes in tree bark to release sugary sap, a substance that makes up 75 percent of their diet.

A number of physical traits differentiate Old World and New World monkeys. Most Old World monkeys have small, curved

① WEEK

▸ Introduced to troop
▸ Crawls on all fours

⑤ WEEKS

▸ Rides on mother's back
▸ Tastes flower buds and leaves
▸ Weight: 24 ounces (680 g)
▸ Height: 7 inches (17.8 cm)

nostrils set close together, while most New World monkeys have broad noses with round nostrils that are set far apart. Old World monkeys often have cheek pouches that can be stuffed with food to be eaten later. And because most Old World monkeys live on the ground, they have hard, hairless pads on their rumps called ischial callosities. Since New World monkeys live in trees, they lack such cheek pouches and seat cushions.

CLOSE-UP
Sleeping

Most monkeys sleep 9 to 11 hours a night. They huddle together, often sitting upright in the forks of tree branches or on cliffs. Chacma baboons have been known to sleep in caves.

FEATURED FAMILY

First Meal

Sitting high in a tree, the mother snow monkey plucks purple wisteria blossoms from a slender branch and pops them into her mouth. They are a delicious treat after a winter spent chewing on tree bark. Her infant is enjoying a different meal: warm milk. His tiny fingers clutch his mother's fur, but he is not yet strong enough to keep from slipping. His mother holds him tightly as he watches her eat. He drinks for several minutes and then falls asleep. He will do little more than eat and sleep for the first week of his life.

Most Old World monkeys have SMALL, CURVED NOSTRILS set close together.

(2) MONTHS

- ► Fur begins to lighten
- ► Explores away from mother
- ► Plays with other infants

CLOSE-UP
Problem-solving

Smart monkeys peer inside trees, lift up rocks
and leaves, and peel back bark in search of
food that may be hidden. Some chase birds
from nests to steal eggs or use sharp rocks to
open shellfish.

CHAPTER TWO
EARLY ADVENTURES

Most monkeys live in groups called troops. The structure of troops varies by species. Large troops of 100 or more female macaques are protected by a dominant male and a few younger males that he selects. Other male macaques hang out together in bachelor troops. Gelada troops on the grasslands of Ethiopia can number as many as 800 animals of all ages and a mix of male and female. Brazil's red-bellied titi (*TEE-tee*) family groups include only two adults and two or three of their young offspring.

Monkeys develop at different rates, depending on the species. Spider monkeys will cling to their mother's belly, nursing and sleeping, for about three months. Then they will begin to look around

---

⑦ MONTHS

▸ Experiences first snowfall
▸ Enters hot springs for the first time
▸ Weight: 2.5 pounds (1.1 kg)

⑪ MONTHS

▸ Begins eating solid foods
▸ Half of diet is vegetation

FEATURED FAMILY

Look Who's Crawling

The infant snow monkey is one week old. His troop members have been patiently waiting to meet him. The mother rejoins the troop near the riverbank and allows the other monkeys to touch the infant. Alarmed, the infant cries out. Then a small cousin—only a year old—reaches out a hand to gently pat the infant's head. The infant's eyes widen. He inhales deeply and makes a squeaking sound. His cousin screeches in reply. The infant pulls away from his mother, and she sets him down in the soft grass. Anxious to play, the infant moves on all fours toward his cousin.

CLOSE-UP
Gripping tails

The tails of most New World monkeys are prehensile, or gripping. Used like another hand, these tails help monkeys climb trees and swing from limb to limb.

with curiosity. Soon, they slowly begin eating solid food and gain enough confidence to leave their mother for short periods to play with other infants. Later, their father will step in to wrestle and play, teaching defense and social skills. Many monkey species are not completely independent of their parents until they are three or four years old.

Communication is vital to building and maintaining relationships and security in a troop. Vocal communication includes hoots, whistles, howls, screeches, and other sounds. Social grooming is also important. Monkeys pick dirt and parasites from each other's fur. This creates or repairs relationships and strengthens friendships and family bonds. Young monkeys learn their place in the social order by watching their mothers and siblings. When they make mistakes, their elders correct their behavior.

 MONTHS

▸ Eats only solid foods

FEATURED **FAMILY**

Give It a Try

After a morning spent eating, the snow monkeys sit in the shade grooming each other. The three-month-old infant clings to his mother's back, watching her run her nimble fingers through the fur of another female. Using her finger-nails, his mother plucks a tick from her companion's skin and pops it into her mouth, crunching it between her front teeth. Still unsure of his goal, the infant mimics his mother and runs his tiny fingers through her fur.

Vocal communication includes
HOOTS, WHISTLES, HOWLS, SCREECHES,
and other sounds.

(2) YEARS

- ▸ Becomes older brother
- ▸ Drops in social rank
- ▸ Weight: 12 pounds (5.4 kg)
- ▸ Height: 13 inches (33 cm)

Hot springs

Established in 1949, Jōshin'etsu-kōgen includes numerous mountains. Some, such as Mt. Asama and Mt. Myōkō, are active volcanoes. They cause water up to 104 ˚F (40 ˚C) to seep up from underground, filling pools known as *onsen*.

CHAPTER THREE
LIFE LESSONS

Environmental factors determine monkeys' diets and behaviors. Nicobar macaques, named for the islands they call home, pluck shellfish from coastal waters. They use rocks to open the shells. Geladas graze for about 10 hours a day, feeding almost solely on grass. Since there is no time for social grooming, geladas "talk" to each other constantly. Most monkeys live in forests where they eat leaves, flowers, fruits, and seeds. To get protein, they may eat grubs, insects, bird eggs, or snails. Baboons, some of the world's largest monkeys, typically live on open savannas and scrubland where vegetation is scarce. They supplement their diets by hunting smaller animals such as birds, hares, baby antelopes, and even smaller monkeys.

(5) YEARS	(6) YEARS
‣ Leaves family troop	‣ Becomes a father for the first time
‣ Joins bachelor troop 20 miles (32.2 km) away	‣ Weight: 26 pounds (11.8 kg)
	‣ Height: 23 inches (58.4 cm)

This Is How It's Done

On an early December morning, the young snow monkey awakes to find his mother covered with snow—the first he's ever seen. He climbs onto her back, and she carries him down the mountain. They join other Japanese macaques already soaking in a steaming pool of water. The mother pulls the baby to her chest as she slips into the pool. The youngster shrieks in surprise, but he soon realizes the warm water feels good. As snow continues to fall, the tiny monkey closes his eyes and rests serenely in his mother's grasp.

Sharing food is a form of social bonding. When a monkey locates food, it will often communicate the find to other members of the troop so that everyone benefits from the resource. But controlling who gets food can be a way of demonstrating power. In a baboon troop, a baboon cannot eat in front of a higher-ranking member without first offering to share. To do so would result in a serious beating by the troop leader. Likewise, the troop leader shares food only with baboons that pledge their loyalty to him. Young baboons quickly learn to share any food they find or catch. Even a fat beetle can be used to earn favor with older baboons.

CLOSE-UP

Power play

Body language is often used to intimidate rivals and avoid fights about food, mates, or leadership. Males with the brightest face or rump colors, the loudest calls, or the fiercest body postures typically win because challengers back down.

⑨ YEARS	⑩ YEARS
▸ Challenges older male for troop leadership ▸ Fathers half of his troop's infants	▸ Successfully defends challenge to leadership

Young monkeys also learn to watch for predators. Leopards can leap 10 feet (3 m) off the ground to grab Old World monkeys out of trees. Chimpanzees launch coordinated attacks on monkeys in Africa. Raptors and pythons ambush unwary monkeys. With razor-sharp, five-inch-long (12.7 cm) claws, harpy eagles snatch New World monkeys right off tree branches. Margays, oncillas, and jaguars—wild cats that hunt at night—grab sleeping monkeys. When monkeys huddle together at night, the youngsters know they must remain in the center of the group for safety.

CLOSE-UP
Weaning

Depending on the species, mother monkeys begin to deny milk to their offspring when they reach one to two years of age. This is called weaning. It can take weeks or months for juveniles to adjust to eating only solid foods.

FEATURED FAMILY

Practice Makes Perfect

The young snow monkey is now two years old. His mother spent the past winter helping him find pine stems, bamboo, and dry mushrooms to eat. Now she will offer her final lessons: finding grubs under tree bark, stealing bird eggs, and selecting the best fruits and nuts. The young monkey must prepare for life without his mother's support, for she is about to give birth again. He must continue improving his food-finding and social-grooming skills if he hopes to move up in the troop's ranks.

MONKEY PREDATORS

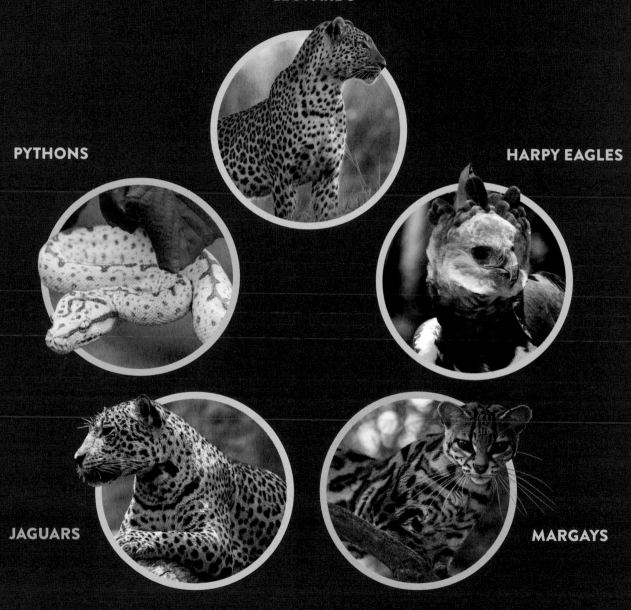

LEOPARDS

PYTHONS

HARPY EAGLES

JAGUARS

MARGAYS

(13) YEARS

(15) YEARS

- ► Breaks tooth
- ► Health begins to fail
- ► Surrenders troop leadership to younger male

- ► End of life

CHAPTER FOUR
MONKEY SPOTTING

Monkeys can live between 15 and 30 years, depending on the species. Since most monkeys become parents by age four to six, and many species can have babies every year or two, troops can grow quickly. When troops become too big, they split up. This way, there will be enough food for everyone in various places. However, humans are interfering with this natural order. Forests are cut down for logging, mining, or expansions of cities and farms, leaving monkeys with ever-shrinking habitats.

The roloway monkey once lived in many forests of Ghana and Côte d'Ivoire, but a 600 percent increase in logging since 1995 has driven this monkey to the brink of extinction. It is now listed among the 25 most endangered primates on Earth by the International Union for Conservation of Nature (IUCN). Five langur species found only in Indonesia, Sri Lanka, and Southeast Asia are also listed as critically endangered. Scientists estimate the species will become extinct within 20 years. Some monkeys, such as the Ka'apor capuchin of Brazil, are so rare that researchers cannot find enough of them for an accurate population count.

Another major threat to monkeys is the bushmeat trade. In this business, wild animals are hunted and sold as food. Hunters typically use snares or traps to catch monkeys or shoot them out of trees. For instance, because of hunting, fewer than 70 mature golden-headed langurs exist in the wild. Even where hunting is illegal, widespread poaching has put many monkey species at risk. The kipunji was discovered in 2003. It lives only in southern Tanzania, where it is threatened by logging and poaching. Researchers estimate that fewer than 1,500 kipunjis remain. The Miss Waldron's red colobus once shared many of the same forests as the roloway monkey, but it is now likely extinct.

One way to protect monkeys from extinction is to learn about how they live and what they need to survive. Scientists study behavior, diet, reproduction, and many other aspects of monkey life to better understand how humans, natural predators, and Earth's changing climate affect monkeys. Despite the efforts of dedicated researchers and conservation groups, monkeys around the world continue to perish. More work must be done—and quickly—if we are to prevent the loss of any more monkey species.

SNAPSHOTS

Found in West Africa, the world's largest monkey is the **mandrill**. Males can weigh 80 pounds (36.3 kg), and their front teeth can be 2.5 inches (6.4 cm) long.

The South American **bald uakari** has an especially powerful lower jaw suited to opening hard, unripe fruits. Most of its diet is seeds from these fruits.

The critically endangered **cotton-top tamarin** lives in forests in South America. All tamarin species suffer from habitat loss.

The **black snub-nosed monkey**, found only in the Chinese province of Yunnan, lives at the highest altitude—above 13,000 feet (3,962 m)—of any primate.

Male **howler monkeys** make sounds that are as loud as a lawn mower. These sounds can be heard up to three miles (4.8 km) away.

Adult **silvery lutungs** of Malaysia and Indonesia are gray, but babies are bright orange. This helps adults quickly locate and rescue babies when danger approaches.

The **proboscis monkey's** nose can be more than five inches (12.7 cm) long. Males with a bigger nose can create a louder call, which gives them a higher social rank.

The endangered **Sclater's guenon** (*guh-NAWN*) is one of the rarest monkeys in Africa. It can be found only in the forests of southern Nigeria.

Central and South America's seven **spider monkey** species have prehensile tails more than three feet (0.9 m) long.

Fewer than 250 **Tonkin snub-nosed monkeys** remain in northern Vietnam. At least half live in the forest of the protected Khau Ca Species and Habitat Conservation Area.

Since the **kipunji's** discovery in 2003, about 1,100 of these monkeys have been spotted in forests covering volcanic mountains in **southern Tanzania**.

Uniquely, the **owl monkey** of South America is active at night. A shy monkey, it feeds at night to avoid competition with more aggressive monkeys.

Living in the deserts of the Horn of Africa and Arabia, the **Hamadryas baboon** is considered the world's most aggressive monkey. Males constantly battle for power.

WORDS to Know

endangered   at risk of dying out completely

extinction   the state of having died off completely

gestation   the period of time it takes a baby to develop inside its mother's body

parasites   animals or plants that live on or inside another living thing (called a host) while giving nothing back to the host; some parasites cause disease or even death

poaching   hunting protected species of wild animals, even though doing so is against the law

primates   animals with large brains and gripping hands; prosimians, monkeys, apes, and humans are primates

savannas   grassy, mostly treeless plains in tropical or subtropical regions

species   a group of living beings with shared characteristics and the ability to reproduce with one another

LEARN MORE

Books

Davey, Owen. *Mad about Monkeys*. London: Flying Eye Books, 2015.

Markle, Sandra. *The Woolly Monkey Mysteries: The Quest to Save a Rainforest Species*. Minneapolis: Millbrook Press, 2019.

Sterry, Paul. *Monkeys & Apes*. Broomall, Penn.: Mason Crest, 2019.

Websites

"Monkey." San Diego Zoo Animals & Plants. https://animals.sandiegozoo.org /animals/monkey.

"Monkey Facts." Animal Facts Encyclopedia. https://www .animalfactsencyclopedia.com/Monkey-facts.html.

"Types of Monkeys." Monkeyworlds. https://www.monkeyworlds.com /types-of-monkeys/.

Documentaries

Farkas, Mitchell. *China's Golden Monkeys*. LIC China/National Geographic Wild, 2014.

Linfield, Mark, and Alastair Fothergill. *Monkey Kingdom*. Disneynature, 2015.

Pontecorvo, Joe. "Snow Monkeys." *Nature*, season 32, episode 10. Rubin Tarrant Productions, 2014.

Note: Every effort has been made to ensure that any websites listed above were active at the time of publication. However, because of the nature of the Internet, it is impossible to guarantee that these sites will remain active indefinitely or that their contents will not be altered.

Visit

ANIMAL TRACKS INC.

Guided educational tours allow visitors a closer look.

10234 Escondido Canyon Road

Agua Dulce, CA 91390

JUNGLE FRIENDS PRIMATE SANCTUARY

This sanctuary houses more than 300 rescued and retired monkeys.

13915 North State Road 121

Gainesville, FL 32653

SMITHSONIAN'S NATIONAL ZOO & CONSERVATION BIOLOGY INSTITUTE

Home to more than a dozen primate species, including Goeldi's and black howler monkeys.

3001 Connecticut Avenue NW

Washington, D.C. 20008

TORONTO ZOO

Features black-handed spider monkeys, marmosets, tamarins, and sakis.

2000 Meadowvale Road

Toronto, ON M1B 5K7

Canada

INDEX